The Demise of a Division
German Infantry Success During the Ardennes Offensive 1944

R.A.B. Bruijns

The Demise of a Division
German Infantry Success
During the Ardennes Offensive 1944

Aspekt Publishers

The Demise of a Division
German Infantry Success During the Ardennes Offensive 1944
© R.A.B. Bruijns
© 2024 Aspekt Publishers |
Amersfoortsestraat 27, 3769 AD, Soesterberg |
info@uitgeverijaspekt.nl www.uitgeverijaspekt.nl

Cover design: Lisa Dijkhuizen
Inside: Paul Timmerman

ISBN: 9789464871081
NUR: 680

All rights reserved. No part of this publication may be reproduced, stored in a retrieval system or transmitted in any form or by any means, electronic, mechanical, photocopying, recording or otherwise, without the prior permission of the publisher.

Insofar as the making of copies from this publication is permitted under Section 16B Copyright Act 1912 jº the Decree of 20 June 1974, Official Gazette 351, as amended by the Decree of 23 August 1985, Official Gazette 471 and Section 17 of the 1912 Dutch Copyright Act, the fees legally due should be paid to Stichting Reprorecht (PO Box 882, 1180 AW, Amstelveen, The Netherlands). For copying part(s) of this publication in anthologies, readers, and other compilations (Section 16 of the Dutch 1912 Copyright Act), please contact the publisher.

Table of contents

Legenda for map icons	6
List of vocabulary and abbrevations	7
Introduction	9
An unpromising mix of men	10
The artillery officer who created an infantry division	17
The American opponent in the Eiffel	22
Volksgrenadiers are being prepared for the offensive	28
The plan and the offensive	35
The nervous days leading up to the offensive	42
December 16, 1944: setbacks on the first day	47
December 17, 1944: the Schneifel trap closes	52
December 18, 1944: the Americans strike back	57
December 19, 1944: the last American convulsion on the Schneifel	62
December 21, 1944: main objective St. Vith	67
Conclusion	73
Literature	77
Register of names	80
Register of places	81

Legenda for map icons

armygroup	×××××
army	××××
armycorps	×××
division	××
division	×
regiment	|||
battalion	||
company	|

⊠	infantry unit
⊠ (with oval)	armoured infantry unit
⌀	reconnaissance unit
○	armour unit
•	artillery unit
◉	assault gun unit
⊓	engineer unit
△	anti-tank unit

List of vocabulary and abbrevations

AD	armoured division
army	military unit consisting of between two to four armycorps
(army)corps	military unit consisting of between two to four divisions, the German army had specialized armoured armycorps: Panzercorps
armygroup	military unit consisting of between two to four armies
battalion	military unit consisting of between 500 and 800 soldiers
brigade	military unit consisting of between 3.000 to 5.000 soldiers
cavalry group	American brigade-sized force of motorized troops, usually deployed as screening forces in quiet sectors between divisions or armycorps
combat command	American ad-hoc command within an armoured division, usually comprised of a tank battalion, an amoured infantry battalion and a mobile artillery battalion (see also: Kampfgruppe). The combat command was designated with a letter [CCA, CCB, CCR(eserve)]
company	military unit consisting of between 100 and 170 soldiers
corps see:	armycorps
division	military unit consisting of between 10.000 and 17.000 soldiers, usually composed of at least three infantry regiments and one artillery regiment
GD	Großdeutschland (Greater Germany: naming convention of the units raised under that name, originally the garrison-regiment of Berlin

GI	literally: government-issue – a colloquial word for American infantry, derived from the stamp 'GI' inside the collar of their uniform.
Heer	German ground forces
HQ	headquarters
ID	Infantry Division
Kampfgruppe	German word for battlegroup, a mixture of different units from different branches to create a strikeforce with all necessary elements (infantry, artillery and/or armour)
Luftwaffe	German airforce
NSDAP	German acronym for National-Socialist German Workers' Party, better known as the Nazi party
Panzerdivision	German word for an armoured division
Panzerfaust	literally: armourfist – German hand-held anti-tank weapon
regiment	military unit consisting of between 2.000 and 3.000 soldiers divided into or three battalions
SS	Schutz-Staffel, literally: security squad – the paramilitary wing of the Nazi party (see: NSDAP), which expanded with a military wing (Waffen-SS). Heinrich Himmler was the chief of the SS.
StuG	Sturmgeschuetz: a German assault gun
Sturmartillerie	German word for the assault gun (see: StuG) branch within the army
U.S.	United States of America
VGD	Volksgrenadier-Division: a German late-1944 type infantry division
Waffen-SS	literally: armed SS – the military wing of the SS, which grew from Hitler's selected elite bodyguard into dozens of frontline divisions
Wehrmacht	regular German ground army, separate from the Luftwaffe (airforce) and the Kriegsmarine (navy)
Westwall	German defense line of bunkers along the border with France and Belgium, also known as Siegfried Line

Introduction

In the literature about the Ardennes offensive of 1944, the attention is invariably focused on the German armoured divisions, such as the audacious dash of Joachim Peiper or how Von Manteuffel's tanks almost reached the Meuse near Dinant. No one thinks of the German infantry when they think of success during this offensive. They are often regarded as the weak link – the foot soldiers who could not keep up with the tanks. This image has been somewhat adjusted by the interesting publication of Douglas Nash (*Victory was beyond their grasp*, 2008) about the 272nd Volksgrenadier-Division. Nash explains in detail how the division was prepared for the Ardennes offensive and achieved modest success early in this offensive, inflicting significant losses on the American 78th Infantry Division (further: ID) in the Huertgen Forest, a vast forest area near Aachen.

The success of the 18th Volksgrenadier-Division at the beginning of the Ardennes offensive deserves a bigger place in the history of the offensive. This division confronted the much stronger and better trained American 106th ID. It managed to largely encircle the Americans within four days and almost completely wipe them off the map – more than 8,000 American soldiers were captured. It was one of the largest mass surrenders in the history of the United States (further: U.S.) Army and the 106th ID had to be rebuilt, almost from the ground up. The defeat of the 106th ID was followed by the capture of St. Vith, which was crucial for the advance of the Wehrmacht (German Army), even more so than Bastogne, because it gave the 6th Panzerarmy a chance to redeploy. For these reasons alone, it is interesting to analyze the confrontation between both divisions and place this battle in the broader context of the Ardennes offensive.

R.A.B. Bruijns

An unpromising mix of men

The origins of the 18th Volksgrenadierdivision go back to the winter of 1942-'43 when the 18th *Luftwaffe Feld-Division* (Airforce Field Division, further: LFD) was formed. The lack of infantry compelled the German High Command to request a transfer of recruits from the *Luftwaffe* (airforce) to the *Heer* (ground army). Luftwaffe-chief Hermann Goering (1893-1946) did not want to cede control of these men and demanded that they were organised as Luftwaffe ground forces under Luftwaffe officers. This way Goering's grenadiers would serve as infantry but remained under the umbrella of the Luftwaffe. Hence the so-called *Luftwaffe Feld-Division* was born.

Luftwaffe-chief Hermann Goering was reluctant to cede troops for the infantry and the result was the *Luftwaffe Field Divisions*.

The formation of Luftwaffe infantry divisions led to all kind of problems. The Luftwaffe could not provide tactical infantry training or infantry officer training. Improvisation made up for lack of resources, and not only regarding the infantry. Artillerists were initially not trained on field guns but were extracted from anti-aircraft forces, and engineers were transfered from construction units. To add insult to injury the artillery was often made up of captured Soviet guns. The LFD looked fine on paper with a full complement of men and equipment, but on closer inspection the division consisted of men with improper training, inadequate officers, and no battlefield experience whatsoever.

All these deficiencies of the 18th LFD and its sister divisions 16th LFD and 17th LFD remained hidden for the moment because these divisions were sent to the Western Front in January 1943 for coastal defense. They enjoyed garrison life undisturbed until the Allied landing in Normandy in June 1944. Initially the LFDs were not committed into battle for fear of poor performance, but soon enough the drain of manpower in Normandy compelled the Germans to do the unthinkable. In the beginning of July, the first such division was put into the line – the 16th LFD. The ferocity of the battle for Caen proved too much for this division and after one month the division was officially disbanded because there were hardly any men left.

The odyssee of the 18th LFD in August-September 1944.

The 18th LFD was moved to the battlefield by the middle of August to defend the river Seine. By then the bulk of the Wehrmacht in Normandy was already close to encirclement in the Falaise pocket and the Allied armoured spearheads seemed unstoppable. On arrival on August 22nd the American infantry had already crossed the Seine and the former airforce men were ordered to drive them back across. This was way beyond the

Luftwaffe Field units were generally well-armed but they suffered from a lack of infantry and officer training.

capabilities of the ill-trained and unexperienced men, and after three days all attacks had been repulsed with heavy losses. The division had been bled white with thousands dead, wounded or taken prisoner. The subsequent chaotic retreat led to further losses by roaming partisans and desertion. By the time the division reached the Belgian border it had the combat strength of a weak battalion, which was encircled in the so-called Mons pocket on September 3rd.

Within less than two weeks from going into action the 18th LFD was defeated, depleted, and surrounded. Nevertheless, its commander Joachim von Tresckow was undettered and led the battered remains of his division out of the pocket on foot. It was not the first time he had seen a unit under his command reduced to ashes. He had commanded the 328th ID on the Eastern Front, which was reduced to a skeleton formation during the bloody battle of Rzhev in the summer of 1942. The rebuilt 328th ID fought in Ukraine during the second half of 1943 until depleted and it was subsequently disbanded. Out of the fire of the Mons pocket the remnants of the 18th LFD jumped into the proverbial frying pan of the Ardennes, where the men were fair game for partisans before reaching the relative safety of the Westwall, better known as the Siegfried Line, on September 18th. Despite his experience and valor (he received the Knight's Cross on September 19th 1944), Von Tresckow was not retained as commander and put (temporarily) in the army reserve instead. It was a sad end, because as a general he saw the demise of three divisions under his command in the past one and a half year.

While the remnants of the division were languishing in the Mons pocket a new 18th Division was born in Denmark. On August 25th 1944 the 571st Volksgrenadier-Division (further: VGD) had been formed near Esbjerg as part of an ambitious scheme by SS-chief Heinrich Himmler. He wanted to invigorate the fighting spirit of the Wehrmacht after the recent setbacks on the Western and Eastern Fronts. The term 'volksgrenadier' (people's grenadier) was to signal a new stage of the war in which the nation ('Volk' in German) would be mobilised to the fullest extent into the army to fight Germany's existential struggle. This meant in reality the mobilization of previously exempted industry workers, entertainers and civil servants, but also the snatching of 16- and 17-year-old boys from the school benches to provide the VGDs a youthful core of physical fit fighters. On September 2nd the embryonic 571st VGD was redesignated 18th VGD as a succession of aforementioned 18th LFD.

Poster presenting the (German) infantry as the 'queen of all arms', the reality was more sobering.

Often a VGD was given a core of experienced troops from a burnt-out division to provide a cadre and instill a kind of divisional pride. The 571st VGD was not blessed with the remnants of the 18th LFD, an ill-trained and inexperienced division which lost its combat capability within a matter of days. It had been on the run during most of its frontline service. Despite the heavy losses the 18th LFD could still provide around 2,500 men to the new division, which was apparently better than nothing. Dietrich Moll, the newly appointed operations officer (equivalent to chief of staff) of the 18th VGD, noted bitterly that there were few decorated soldiers and officers in the division even though Germany was in the sixth year of the war. The combat elements of the division were replenished by 5,000 recruits and 3,000 men transferred from the navy and air force.

In a twist of irony, the 18th VGD was in September 1944 in a similar situation as the 18th LFD had been in January 1943. Most men came from other branches of the German armed forces and were not trained infantrymen, nor were the officers educated frontline commanders. Despite the German propaganda that the infantry was the *'Koenigin aller Waffen'* (queen of all army-branches), transfer to the infantry was not seen as a promotion by naval and air force service personnel at this stage of the war. It was an act of desperation by an army that was losing infantry faster than it could train them. The new recruits for the division were also not fresh, enthusiastic young men, but largely middle-aged family men. Nor had they had any infantry training under their belt because Germany had no conscription between 1919 and 1935. The Ministry of Propaganda noted on October 23rd that the German public deplored the new wave of mobilisation and regarded the men called up for the VGDs as cannonfodder. What followed was a media campaign to assure the public that the VGDs were outfitted with the best available armaments.

At the beginning of September 1944, the 18th VGD must have given a dismal impression as a heap of hopeless men from a wide variety of manpower sources with the chaos of ranks and uniforms entailed to that. Morale was low after the stream of bad tidings from the front and the relentless bombardments on German cities. But this mix of demoralized survivors of the rout in France, disgruntled transferred naval and air force personnel, and cynical middle-aged recruits had to be forged into a deployable infantry division by a new commander in a matter of weeks. This truly Herculean task fell to Colonel Guenther Hoffmann-Schoenborn (hereinafter: Hoffmann) on September 15th 1944.

The artillery officer who created an infantry division

Mid-September 1944 Guenther Hoffmann drove up to the training camp of the 18th VGD in the Danish region of Jutland. He was probably disappointed to be appointed commander of an infantry division, particularly of such low repute and little promise, as he had recently completed training to become a panzercommander. Hoffmann was originally an artillery officer, but in 1940 his fate became linked to the new branch of the *Sturmartillerie*. The German *Sturmgeschuetz* (assault gun, further: StuG) is often lumped in with other German tanks, as it is a tracked vehicle with a gun, but it was actually part of the artillery. Unlike the tank corps, a mobile artillery unit provided direct fire support to the infantry in the front line. It also turned out to be a very effective anti-tank weapon due to its low silhouet. Over 10,000 StuGs were produced during the war, making it the most-produced German armoured fighting-vehicule during World War Two. This unassuming infantry-support vehicle will play a major role in the success of the 18th VGD in December 1944 as we shall see.

Guenter Hoffmann (born in 1905 in Posen, nowadays: Poznań) began his career in the Sturmartillerie as a commander of Sturmartillerie-Abteilung 191 in the autumn of 1940 and made a splash with this unit. In the spring of 1941, his unit was decisive in overcoming the Metaxas defense line in Greece and advancid along the Greek coast beyond Thermopylae Pass, known as the place where during Antiquity the Spartans fought to death against the

Guenther Hoffmann-Schoenborn made a dashing career as a commander of an assault gun unit, earning the Knight's Cross.

Persian army. For his services during this campaign, Hoffmann received on May 14th 1941 the Knight's Cross, the highest German reward for valor. His unit was part of the German invasion of Soviet-Russia and he reached the gates of Moscow with his assault gun unit in December 1941, where he was seriously wounded. In this light of Hoffmann's dashing career so far, it is incomprehensible that an author such as Bruce Quarrie describes this officer as 'without any combat experience' in the Osprey order-of-battle book on the 5th Panzerarmy (2000, 79).

Hoffmann's frontline career was cut short at the end of 1941 due to his wounds, but he was awarded the Oak Leafs with the Knight's Cross on December 31st 1941 as an acknowledgement of his performances. His wounds did however not mean the end of his army career. His impressive combat and command record ensured that he became an officer in the training of the Sturmartillerie, which was significantly expanded during that period – within a year the number of operational StuGs more than doubled. His transfer was also a promotion – officers with a good frontline servicerecord were assigned as training officers. Hoffmann served as a

The assault gun StuG III was one of the most produced German tracked vehicles during the war.

training officer for more than two years until he was assigned to the army reserve, the reservoir of officers, in July 1944. In that capacity, as a colonel, he trained to become a general of a panzerdivision, which was somewhat in line with his experience with assault guns. Within the Sturmartillerie the largest unit was the brigade, so there was no room for promotion. Germany's armoured force was on the other hand based on the concept of the panzerdivision and considered an elite force. His dreams of becoming of panzercommander were however dashed in September 1944.

The marker of the 18th Volksgrenadierdivision, which was painted on their vehicles.

The nomination of Hoffmann as commander of the 18th VGD was part of a pattern in which young promising officers of relatively junior rank were entrusted with the leadership of a Volksgrenadier division. For example, the commanders of the 26th VGD and 272nd VGD were also colonels, bearers of the Knight's Cross, and around forty years of age. Since many former exemptees were drafted into the VGD, the divisioncommander had often the same age as a significant portion of his soldiers. It is difficult to determine their political beliefs, but commanders like Hoffmann had the officer profile that National-Socialists liked: young, highly decorated, non-noble and *Draufgaenger* (daredevil, i.e. leading from the front). After the assassination attempt on Hitler on July 20th 1944, political reliability was a big plus for promotions. Hoffmann apparently fitted the bill, and he was shortlisted for command of a VGD, Himmler's pet project as we have seen above. At this stage he did not know, but the VGDs were intended as assault divisions for the upcoming offensive.

The timetable for whipping the VGDs into shape was measured in weeks, not months. With limited time at hand, Hoffmann immediately set to work to prepare the division for combat as quickly as possible upon his arrival at the training camp of the 18th VGD. The first thing he did was set up an internal officer training course and sift through his officer base. This was one of the division's original defects, which had caused the premature demise of many LFDs, and Hoffmann was dead set on tackling it before the division would go to the front. The former Luftwaffe officers were often found unsuitable for frontline command despite their formal rank, and relieved of their duties. Hoffmann set up a rigorous examination for potential commanders and selected the most suitable commanders for his regiments, battalions and companies. As it later turned out, this was an important ingredient for the division's success, although each company had on average just one officer.

German soldiers on the train in Denmark during the occupation.

Not only the commanding officers of the 18th VGD were reshuffled, but also the structure as a whole. The division would not inherit the regimental numbers of the 18th LFD or even the regimental numbers of the provisional 571st VGD, but it was rebuilt from the ground up with relative low regimental numbers for its infantry regiments – 293rd, 294th and 295th. Despite the 'inheritance' of the divisional number from the puny 18th LFD, everything was done to wipe out any further reference to it. The 'reborn' 18th was to have a new 'esprit de corps' under the command of Hoffmann, to the furtest extent possible. The mood within the division changed as a result with his vigorous drive to make the most of his command, like he has always done. For two and a half years he had been whipping into shape recruits for the *Sturmartillerie*, and now he used this training experience to do the same with the 18th VGD.

It was however not only a matter of instructing and disciplining the new recruits, but also rewarding the old hands. The best way to drive up morale among the rank and file was the awarding of decorations to the veterans of France. A fair amount of them got the infantry assault award, the wound badge or even the iron cross in some cases. It restored their pride and selfconfidence after the defeat in France, and it set an example for the new arrivals. The freshly minted veterans got status and authority within the new units and would often serve as NCOs to lead the newbies into battle. For the new recruits, the emphasis was on field training and familiarizing themselves with their weapons. This went relatively quick, although training with machine guns and communication methods was not yet complete when the division was deemed ready. Ready in this context meant suitable for limited defensive duties.

Time was not on the side of the 18th VGD, because the Allies were literally standing on Germany's doorstep and the fragile new frontline was holding on by a thread. The division had had only 50 days of training (if we count weekends in), or the equivalent of seven weeks. The 18th VGD had to complete its training on the job. On October 22nd 1944, the first trains left Denmark for the Eiffel on the German-Belgian border near St. Vith. There the 18th VGD had to relieve the remnants of the 2nd SS-Panzerdivision. This exhausted division had had to cover the front since September 1944 while awaiting relief to replenish its losses in the hinterland and train for the upcoming Ardennes offensive.

The American opponent in the Eiffel

The Eiffel sector was one of the few places along the German border where the Americans managed to breach the German defensive line in the beginning of September 1944. They had crossed the river Our and occupied the Westwall bunkers on the ridge known as the Schneifel. The Schneifel ran parallel to the Belgian-German border and is topped by the Schwarzer Mann, the third highest peak in the Eiffel region. This gave the Americans a good basis for defense in this sector – any frontal German attack would be an uphill struggle, and the Americans could take shelter in the bunkers from artillery fire. The Americans found it to be a good location for resting worn-down divisions and let the fresh troops get accustomed to the routine of frontline life. This mentality turned out to be a flaw in the thinking of the US military leadership – a front unit must take into account that it could be exposed to enemy aggression at any time.

By the end of October 1944, the American 2nd ID was in this front sector, and it was not clear to the Germans whether the Americans of this division would attack. It was therefore understandable that the depleted 2nd SS-Panzerdivision wanted to be relieved by the 18th VGD as soon as possible. To the irritation of Waffen-SS general Heinz Lammerding (1905-1971), Hoffmann demanded that the takeover of the positions be carried out systematically, even if this would result in a delay of several days. In order to avoid interdicting artillery fire, the Americans should not get wind of the troop movements. In turn, the Volksgrenadiers felt relief when the American 2nd ID was relieved by the inexperienced American 106th ID in early December 1944. By that time it seemed at face value that both parties had downgraded their presence in this frontsector by inexperienced divisions which were getting accustomed to frontline duty in a quiet sector.

SS-general Heinz Lammerding was dismayed with the slow extracting of his exhausted troops in October 1944.

The 106th ID was a good example of how the American land forces organized and trained their divisions before they were deployed to the front. This division was recruited entirely from young men in the spring of 1943. The division was gradually and carefully built up and trained for a year and a half, with units performing maneuvers at company, battalion, regimental and ultimately division level. The men were fully familiarized with their weapons and the tactical and operational tasks of their division. The Germans could only dream of such an extensive training program at the end of 1944 – a German division at that stage was prepared in a matter of weeks, as we have seen.

It should however be noted that the 106th ID had to deal with a high degree of personnel turnover during its formation and training. For example, between April and August 1944 the division had to give up 7,000 men to replace losses of divisions in the field, for which the division received replacement personnel. These personnel came from a variety of sources – 2,500 from support forces, 1,500 from other divisions, 1,200 from a specialized program for intelligent soldiers, and 1,100 from an air force program. In that sense, the 106th ID was eventually as much a hodgepodge as the 18th VGD, with the important difference that most of the soldiers of the 106th ID had already completed basic military training.

Similar to the 18th VGD the American men transferred from other branches to the infantry were not happy about it. Usually, the branches would cast out its misfits, but also because a transfer to the infantry was being regarded as the most dirty and dangerous job with the most propability to be killed, or worse: wounded. The infantry was generally regarded as not prestigious, even within the ground forces. That's because the U.S. Army distributed soldiers largely on the basis of the *Army General Classification Test* (AGCT). This was done to redirect intelligent people to specific branches, where their skills and education were needed. After the officer candidate schools and specialized technical branches (engineers, artillery, etc.) had skimmed off the cream, the 'leftovers' went to the infantry. This rigorous selection was logical and efficient, but a side-effect was that men with low scores felt unappreciated and left to do the 'dirty jobs'. This low regard was also handicapped by a general lack of regimental history and pride, with some exceptions of course. The modern

Volksgrenadiers were gradually inserted into the line in October 1944.

U.S. Army had been so small before both world wars that there was hardly any unit tradition or cohesion, except perhaps for units stemming from the state-based National Guard. New infantry divisions and regiments were however all formed from the same mold and numbered in serials, like standardized products coming off a conveyor belt. The term 'GI' (government issue, army slang for 'soldier') encapsulated the low self-esteem in sardonic humor: they were as unassuming as their (government issued) uniforms, and just as expendable.

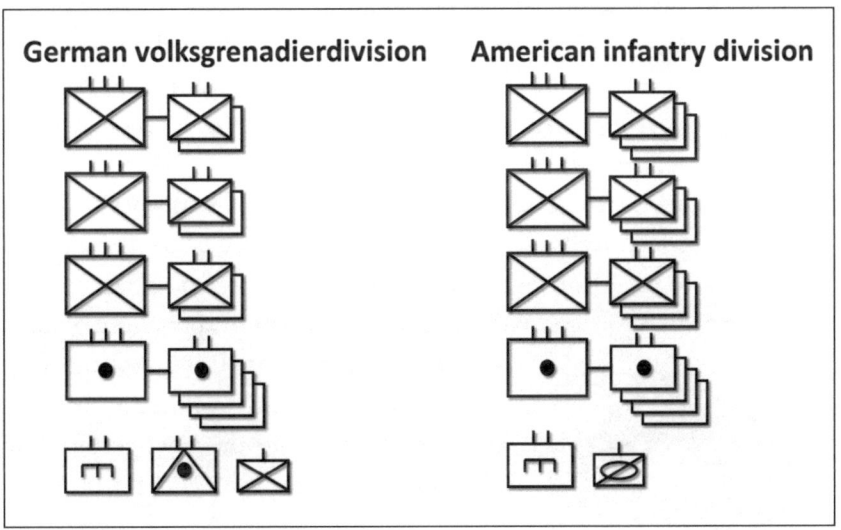

Order of battle of the opposing divisions.

Despite the heavy losses in the autumn battles of 1944 the U.S. Army had still a distinct numerical advantage over the Wehrmacht. An American infantry division consisted of three infantry regiments with three battalions each. A Volksgrenadier division on the other hand could field three infantry regiments with only two battalions each. This meant that a German Volksgrenadier division had at least one third less frontline troops than an American infantry division. In the case of the 106th ID, there was an enormous preponderance of artillery, as eight battalions of field artillery from the VIII Corps were at the division's disposal. This meant a tripling of the normal amount of artillery, as the division itself already had four battalions of artillery. The artillery was due to the above-mentioned policy of selecting intelligent men for the job, one of the strongest assets of the U.S. Army. Due to good mathematics skills American artillerists could quickly put very concentrated and very accurate artilleryfire, and many German attacks were broken by artillery up as a result.

The 106th ID's greatest weakness was its inexperienced officer cadre. Unlike the Wehrmacht, the American army did not provide a core of experienced officers and men when creating a new division. Alan W. Jones (1894-1969), commander of the 106th ID, had served as a captain during the First World War, but he had no frontline experience during that war. In the interwar period he rose through the ranks to colonel, reaching the rank of major general in March 1943. It is somewhat surprising that the American army, which had been at war for three years by December 1944, had no experienced generals to spare for a new division. This also applied to other newly raised divisions. For example, the American 99th ID in the Ardennes sector was also led by an inexperienced general. American divisions were built from the ground up with inexperienced officers and men. There was no question of a system of transferring experienced officers, as the Germans knew it. This meant that new tactics stemming from frontline experience were not passed on to the new recruits, and that officers were as green as their men.

The American general Alan W. Jones was a professional soldier since 1917, but had no battlefield experience.

On December 10th, the 106th ID arrived in Belgium on its way to the front. In a 1992 study project by the American Army on the 106th ID, it was pointed out that the men of the 106th ID had suffered greatly under the conditions of the move from England to Belgium. They had had to camp in open fields in England during heavy autumn rain. Subsequently they had to wait for disembarkation in France for four days on ships on a turbulent sea. Once disembarked, they had to camp in tents in the mud again. Last but not least, they were moved to Belgium in open topped trucks in freezing weather. When the division arrived at the front, the men were numb from the wet and cold. It certainly didn't do morale any good. On the other hand, in the Wehrmacht comfort was also not a high priority, and transport by truck was a luxury for the German soldier at the end of 1944 due to acute fuel shortages.

Volksgrenadiers are being prepared for the offensive

By the time 18th VGD was transported to the Western Front, the frontline had largely solidified after the crisis at the beginning of September. This was underlined in the German propaganda, which trumpeted the arrival of the fresh VGDs at the front in a concerted media campaign in the German newspapers. The VGDs were supposedly stronger in firepower and in fighting spirit, and it was suggested in German propaganda that the Allies could feel the stiffening of the frontline due to their arrival. This propaganda was however not widely believed, as even a large part of the German people felt that the men mobilised for these divisions were pitiful cannonfodder. Despite the fact that the VGDs had a larger distribution of automatic weapons, the division itself was not much different from a Wehrmacht division in 1944. The U.S. Army was not much impressed by the VGDs and the deployment of these divisions was not a cause of anxiety. This was also the case when the 18th VGD was detected in the Eiffel sector by the end of October 1944.

When the 18th VGD was deployed in the Eiffel, the frontsector it was supposed to cover was far too large for its size. A German division was expected to be able to cover a maximum of nine kilometers (5.6 miles) of front against a conventional attack, but the 18th VGD had to cover no less than nineteen kilometers (11.8 miles). This meant that the division could not occupy a continuous front line and that all available battalions -apart from the artillery- had to be deployed at the front, including the engineer battalion. During the period the 18th VGD arrived at the front, all available German infantry units were directed to the meat grinder of the Huertgen Forest near Aachen to stop the American advance. Since the 18th VGD was considered only capable of limited defense, this unit was not deployed in the Huertgen Forest, but relegated to this relatively quiet front sector. This gave the soldiers time to get used to life on the frontline, and the opportunity to resume training as best as they could. For the latter task, a training company was established, which rotated men from frontline units in order to improve tactical skills and conduct training on at least company level.

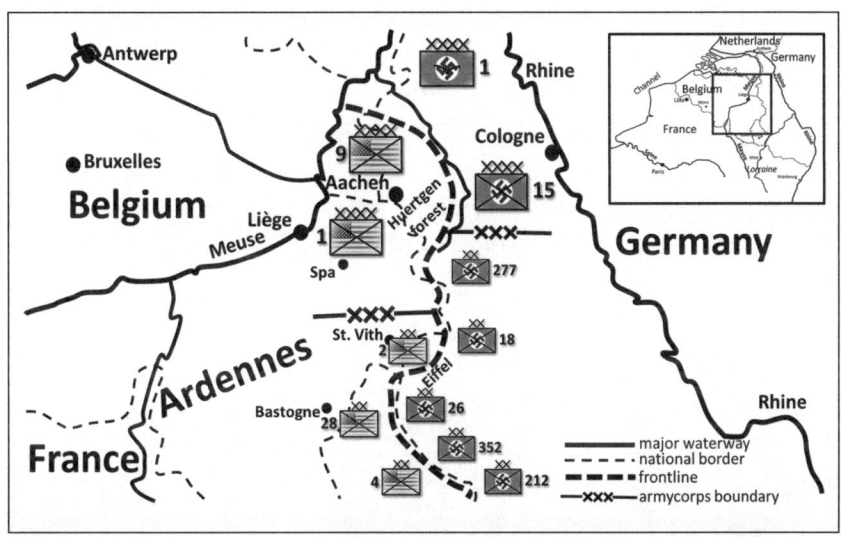

The military situation in the Ardennes and Aachen sector by the end of November 1944.

Paradoxically, the quiet front sector did not give the 18th VGD any real opportunity for idleness, because the division had to control an increasing frontsector. In early November the division took over four kilometers (2.5 miles) on the left flank and in early December nine kilometers (5.6 miles) on the right flank was taken over from the 277th VGD. All in all, the 18th VGD had to cover 32 kilometers (19.9 miles) of front, an almost impossible task. It ensured however that the infantry did not remain passive in their foxholes, because the frontline had to be covered as best as possible through intensive patrolling. This gave the men valuable experience for the coming offensive, such as moving unnoticed through the terrain in the vicinity of the enemy. It also gave the division useful intelligence about the positions of the American units.

The Americans apparently paid less attention to patrolling the front line, otherwise they would have known how few German soldiers were in front of them in the sector covered by the 18th VGD. Hoffmann knew how dangerous this situation was and he did not want to make the enemy wiser than he was in any way. For this reason, he was very upset about a relatively small number of deserters. He issued a message to his soldiers expressing his displeasure with the military information the deserters had provided to the enemy and threatened that their families would pay for their behavior. He knew that it was impossible to stop his men from defecting during the many patrols, but the fear of retribution against relatives apparently had a chilling effect on potential deserters. By late October 1944 discipline was largely restored in the Wehrmacht, but the information of only a few talkative deserters could be sufficient to reveal the division's dire frontline situation.

The 18th VGD spent a lot of time patrolling prior to the Ardennes offensive.

Despite these unfavorable circumstances, Hoffmann managed to upgrade the status of the 18th VGD to 'suitable for limited attacks' during November 1944. His superiors were so satisfied with his results that they promoted him to the rank of major general on December 1st 1944. This promotion was no doubt celebrated with a toast in the headquarters (HQ) of his immediate superior, general Walter Lucht of the LXVI Armycorps. Lucht took the opportunity to take Hoffmann aside to discuss the possibilities of an offensive in this sector. Lucht instructed Hoffmann

Walther Lucht was the superior officer of Hoffmann, but relied on him to devise a plan to defeat the Americans in the Eiffel.

The MP44 was among the first mass-produced assault rifles and widely distributed among volksgrenadiers.

to draw up a plan to encircle the American troops on the Schneifel and capture the town of St. Vith. This was a very ambitious plan, even with the support of the newly arrived 62nd VGD. Since the battle-hardened American 2nd ID was still in this sector at the time, such an attack would realistically have little chance of success, especially when the American artillery would come into play. The American 2nd ID would later show what it was capable of during the Ardennes Offensive by stopping the much stronger German attack on the Elsenborn Ridge.

Hoffmann knew which division was opposite of his, but once again proved to be the type of officer the regime could count on. He did not protest that this operation was beyond the capabilities of his division, but he worked energetically to get his division into shape within the two weeks between the briefing and the attack. He selected companies for a special crash course in assault tactics and ordered exercises with live ammunition to mimic battlefield conditions as close as possible. It was also realized higher up that a pure infantry attack was more likely to succeed if it was supported by sufficient firepower and for that reason StuG-Brigade 244 was added to the 18th VGD. The StuGs would give the infantry the direct firepower it would need to break American defenses and as a safeguard against potential

The coat of arms of the Sturmgeschuetz Brigade 244.

American armoured forces. It was a Godsend for Hoffmann, because the combination of StuGs and infantry was precisely the type of operations in which he was experienced as the former commander of StuG-unit.

The StuG became the indispensable ally of the German infantry during the war.

StuG-Brigade 244 was an experienced unit, which was formed in June 1941, just before the German invasion of the Soviet-Russia and it followed the German advance until the Wolga in 1942. After its encirclement at Stalingrad, it was destroyed there during the winter of 1942-'43. In the spring of 1943 it was reconstituted and again sent to the Eastern Front until destroyed with the demise of Armygroup Centre during the summer of 1944. The StuG-Brigade was again rebuilt and sent to the Western Front to buttress the front of the 15th Army in the Netherlands. In November 1944 the battered StuG-Brigade 244 was evacuated over the river Meuse together with the remnants of the 15th Army. When the brigade arrived in the sector of LXVI Armycorps in the beginning of December it had only 14 StuGs out of a supposed strength of 45 StuGs. It had in other words the brigade had the strength of just one battery instead of three. Nevertheless, even though it was understrength the brigade would be an indispensable tool for the upcoming assault of the 18th VGD.

The plan and the offensive

The Germans did not completely face a completely unexperienced foe. Contrary to major general Alan W. Jones the American VIII Corps commander Troy H. Middleton (1889-1976) had extensive experience as a both a junior officer during World War One and as an armycorps-commander since June 1944. Middleton had been teaching at the War College between the wars and came out of retirement to command the 45th ID, which he led in Sicily and at Salerno in 1943.

Major general Middleton was a professional soldier with sound experience in his role as corps commander.

At the eve of the Ardennes offensive, he had led VIII Corps for six months. From October 4th this corps had been stationed in the Eiffel to screen this quiet sector between the raging battles for Aachen and Metz. As a result, VIII Corps became the Cinderella of the U.S. 1st Army, where divisions were rotated in and out for rest and refit. On top of that, the armycorps never had enough forces to properly defend the 120-kilometer (74.5 miles) sector. By the end of November Middleton had two experienced but badly battered divisions under his command – the 28th ID and 2nd ID.

Middleton was aware of the vulnerable position of his forces on the Schneifel, which was a bulge in the German line. He took advantage of the relief of the 2nd ID by the 106th ID to raise this issue with Courtney B. Hodges (1887-1966) of the 1st U.S. Army in Spa. However, his appeal was rejected – the Schneifel could not be given up to the Germans without a fight. The Schneifel Ridge was one of the few breaches in the Westwall, which caused headaches for Americans elsewhere, like near Aachen and in the Saar. The 106th ID was therefore implicitly given the mission to stick to the Schneifel. The importance of the ridge was underlined by the fact that the division occupied the ridge with no fewer than two of its three regiments. There were however advantages: the division was able to use the dominant position on the ridge and the bunkers of the Westwall for defense. What could go wrong in such a favorable position?

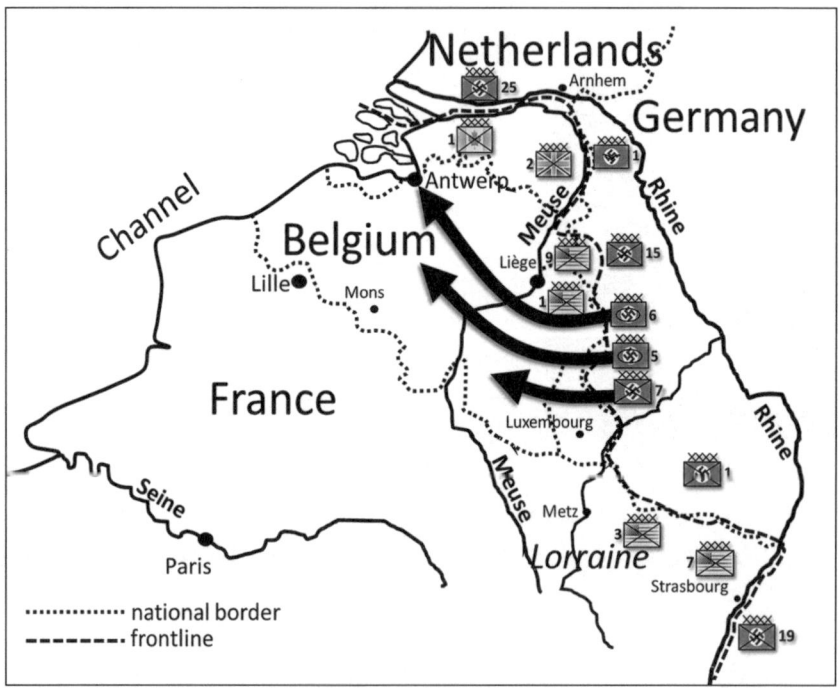

The disposition of the armies on the Western Front in December 1944 and the plan of the Ardennes offensive.

In order to have a better understanding of the context of the position of the 18th VGD in the Ardennes offensive, we need to have a look at 5th Panzerarmy. North of 5th Panzerarmy was 6th Panzerarmy, the main point of effort of the Ardennes offensive with no less than four SS-Panzerdivisions. The 5th Panzerarmy had to protect the southflank of this army while advancing parallel to it to the Meuse. The 5th Panzerarmy itself consisted of three armycorps – two panzer-armycorps and one infantry-armycorps. The two panzer-armycorps were focused on the crossraods of Bastogne and Houffalize, while the (LXVI) infantry-armycorps would focus on St. Vith. The LXVI Armycorps had two VGDs (and a weak StuG-Brigade) for this purpose. The reason for the absence of major armoured units in this sector was simply the lack of hardened roads on the east-west axis.

The StuGs on transport. The Germans transported their heavy equipment by rail to the Ardennes.

The American defensive position on the Schneifel seemed unaissable, but there was a weakness in the form of a single direct supply line, namely the bridge over the river Our in the town of Schoenberg. The river Our was a barrier and all traffic to and from the Schneifel had to pass through this funnel. Hoffmann was well aware of Schoenberg's operational importance. A frontal attack to capture head-on the Schneifel would certainly end in a bloodbath, but if he managed to bypass the Schneifel by advancing through the rugged terrain to the left and right of the Schneifel, he would have a chance to seize Schoenberg before American reinforcements would arrive, or the 106th ID could retreat. Once he had captured Schoenberg, the American troops on the Schneifel would be cut off from their supply of food and ammunition.

Hoffmann's reason for choosing the right flank of the Schneifel was because his patrols had discovered that this was the sector between the American 106th ID and the 14th Cavalry Group. The line is weakest on these boundaries between two commands, and Hoffmann decided to concentrate two of his three regiments here (294th and 295th), as well as the StuG-Brigade 244. His third regiment (293rd) had to reach the Our from the left flank of the Schneifel to prevent the Americans from coming to the aid of their troops on the Schneifel with the third regiment (424th) of the 106th ID. In other words, the 18th VGD would concentrate all its front troops in two axis of attack and thus completely empty the front line opposite the Schneifel of combat units – there was only a token force: the training company. The sister-division 62nd VGD would advance south in support of 18th VGD, but would have no major role in Hoffmann's plan to encircle the bulk of the American 106th ID.

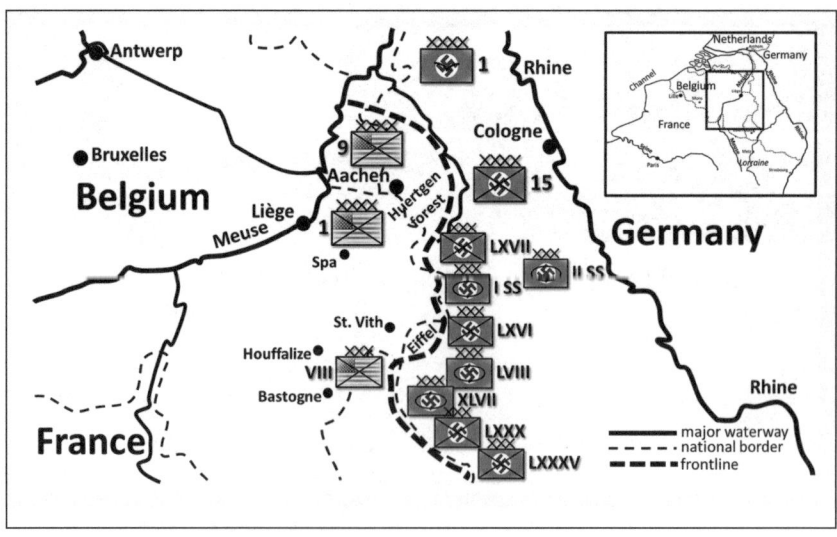

Disposition of the German and Allied armies and armycorps on the eve of the Ardennes offensive.

Two things were essential to the success of Hoffmann's plan. First, the attack had to be carried out quickly to prevent American forces from bringing reinforcements via Schoenberg. After all, the American army was fully motorized, while the German volkgrenadiers had to reach their goal on foot on muddy roads through hills and forests. Secondly, the two

American regiments on the Schneifel had to remain there, because the Germans would not be able to defend Schoenberg against attacks from two sides. There was even the danger that the main German force would become isolated if the American regiments counterattacked from the Schneifel.

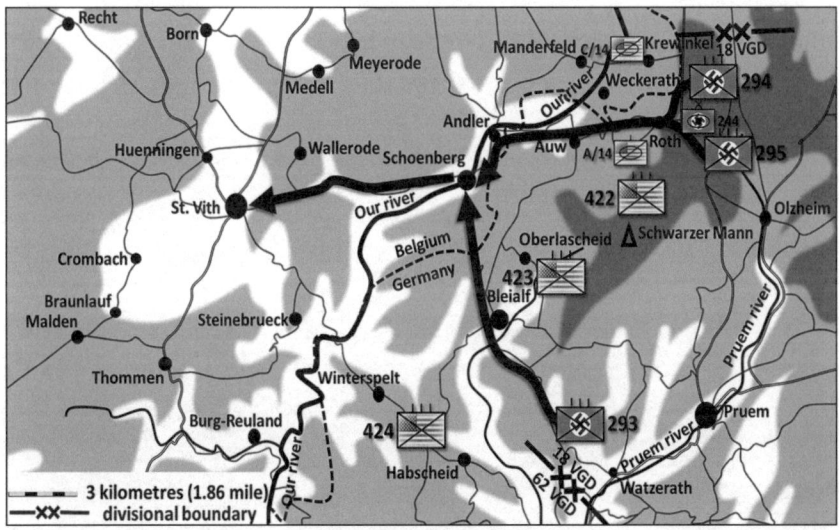

The battleplan of the 18th VGD prior to the Ardennes offensive.

The attack plan was drawn up in great secrecy and was ambitious – Schoenberg was to be captured on December 17th and the division was to reach St. Vith on December 18th. The rank and file were only informed of the offensive on the eve of the offensive. Hoffmann's division was nevertheless probably the best prepared unit of the Ardennes offensive – the division was familiar with the terrain, it had a detailed attack plan, and it had trained for weeks for this attack. Most divisions earmarked for the Ardennes would not appear on the front line until the eve of the offensive. They often had to do without a detailed tactical plan of attack and extensive terrain knowledge. For them it was largely a leap in the dark.

This unfamiliarity with the battlefield and the inexperience of the other infantrydivisions becomes clear when we look at their arrivals. The 26th VGD arrived one month after 18th VGD, and the 62nd VGD was only fully deployed by December 14th. The 560th VGD had to come all the way from Norway and only two of its three regiments managed to reach the startline on December 16th, the remaining troops trickling in during the offensive. The panzerdivisions fared even worse – the Panzer Lehr Division only arrived on December 10th and the 116th Panzerdivision on December 12th. The 2nd Panzerdivision was the exception and had been in the region since their arrival in September 1944. In this light the 18th VGD was lucky to have already spent at least more than six weeks in the frontline.

An aerial photograph of St.Vith in 1940, the goal of 18th VGD in 1944.

Although Hoffmann's attack plan was well thought out, it was also an all-or-nothing plan. If the division was stopped unexpectedly while carrying out its maneuver, it would be in a very vulnerable position and exposed to the dreaded American artillery. The division would have also its own communication problems, as the division commander was determined to lead the offensive from the front on the right flank. This meant that if the division commander was killed or captured, the division would be leaderless with all the consequences that would entail. Furthermore, a commander in the vanguard would have difficulty anticipating setbacks elsewhere. In other words, the attack had to go completely according to plan, or it would lead to disaster and the possible demise of the division.

The nervous days leading up to the offensive

On December 10th 1944 Hoffmann informed his regimental commanders of the upcoming Ardennes offensive. It was the same day that the American 106th ID arrived in the sector of the 18th VGD. The German listening posts soon reported this troop movement, so that the German commanders quickly realized what kind of unit was in front of them. It would be the first major battle for both divisions and therefore a test of their training and their commanders. Although the training of the American soldiers was considerably better, the German soldiers had at least some experience compared to their American counterparts, and this increased the chance of success of Hoffmann's plan.

A week before the planned begin of the Ardennes offensive, the countdown had begun and concrete preparations for the advance of the 18th VGD were put into effect. For example, a special well-camouflaged bridge was built to allow the StuGs to reach the front on the day of the attack. Furthermore, a military police unit was deployed near Pruem to manage the traffic situation during the offensive. The limited and poor road network should not lead to an inextricable tangle of vehicles and units from different directions. This indicated that division HQ was keen that everything should proceed in an orderly manner and that nothing should be left to chance. For example, Hoffmann personally oversaw the movement of the StuG-Brigade to the assembly sector for the attack. All these precautions were in contrast to the situation in the sector of the 1st SS-Panzerdivision, where the traffic soon became jammed after the kick-off of their attack due to the lack of such preparations.

Meanwhile, there was an apparent calm in the sector of the 18th VGD as not to alarm the Americans. In the neighboring sector, preparations were much noisier. From December 14th onward on both sides of the LXVI Armycorps tanks and armored vehicles advanced to their assembly

Dwight D. Eisenhower, the supreme commander of the Allied forces in Western Europe.

sectors directly behind the front line. The roar of tank engines and the squeaks of tanktracks echoed in the Ardennes hills, much to the despair of the staff officers of the 18th VGD – would the Americans be alerted to the impending attack and strengthen their front line in the days before the beginning of the offensive? The sounds of tanks and tracked vehicles certainly alarmed the American intelligence officers of the 106th ID. However, they were told by the U.S. 1st Army HQ in Spa not to get too excited because the Germans were probably playing gramophone records with tank sounds...

Why was the intelligence from the 106th ID ignored? Dwight D. Eisenhower (1890-1969), the Supreme Allied Commander of the Allied Expeditionary Force (SHAEF), declared in hindsight that he had made a calculated risk by the overextension of VIII Corps in the Ardennes. The Germans seemed to be exhausted by the autumn battles of attrition, and the rugged terrain and poor road network of the Ardennes made it look impassable in the dead of winter. Eisenhower's assessment was shared by his subordinate Omar Bradley (1893-1981), the commander of the 12th Armygroup under which the U.S. 1st Army ressorted. Bradley did however not make any precaution to anticipate a German attack in the Ardennes offensive. The intelligence reports pointing to a German troop built-up in the region were just ignored, because it interfered with the decision of high command to contend with a token force to defend this sector.

Omar Bradley, who was aware of the calculated risk in the Ardennes but did not prepare a back-up plan.

On the eve of the Ardennes offensive, the LXVI Armycorps was flanked by the armored troops of the 5th Panzer Army on the left and the 6th Panzer Army on the right flank. The division was thus covered for attacks from the south and north on both the left flank and the right flank. It was anticipated that these attacks would outrun the footsoldiers of the 18th VGD. On the left flank, the 62nd VGD would support with the attack of their sisterdivision by distracting the third regiment of the American 106th ID, preventing this unit from coming to the aid of the rest of the division on the Schneifel. On the right flank, the Ist SS-Panzercorps with two SS-panzerdivisions and three infantry divisions would drive a deep wedge through the American lines at great speed, or at least that was the plan.

The moment for the attack was determined on the basis of the intelligence that the 18th VGD had collected in the weeks before the Ardennes offensive. For example, the Germans had noticed that the Americans kept 'office hours', meaning that activities were limited to the period between nine and five o'clock with a break for lunch. The Americans also preferred to send shells rather than troops to cover the front line, as the former were plentiful in supply – it was not uncommon to fire thousands of shells on a calm day to discourage the Germans from approaching the American lines. As a result, American patrol activities were limited and, especially after nightfall, the Americans no longer came out of their foxholes. It was therefore decided to launch the attack in the earliest morning before dawn.

SS-units were supposed to be the vanguard, but underperformed in the Ardennes offensive.

Contrary to the German attack doctrine the soldiers of the 18th VGD would advance without a preliminary artillery barrage. This was a risk, because if the Americans would be alarmed and on their posts before the Germans could reach their positions, they could be in for a hail of bullets, or worse: caught in the open by the acurate artillery fire. The preliminary artillery barrage was deemed counterproductive, because it would only alarm the Americans that an attack was imminent. Part of the plan was that the Americans in this sector should be lulled in a sense of security, not be alarmed. Another reason was that a large portion of Hoffmann's volksgrenadiers had by now become experienced patrollers and they would put their experience to good use by infiltrating the American lines before dawn. By the time the Americans would find out what was happening, the German soldiers would have reached the American rear. Silence and stealth was essential for the attack to succeed.

At the last moment the 'neighbors' of the Ist SS-Panzercorps seemed to throw a spanner in the works by launching an overwhelming but inaccurate artillery bombardment on the American positions in the neighboring sector at half past five, but by then Hoffmann's volksgrenadiers were already on their way for one and a half hour. The bombardment was in any case a rude awaking of the frontline which had been in a slumber since the end of September 1944. The Americans in the frontline were under no illusions of the scale of the German offensive, although it took a while before this news trickled through to higher HQ. The surprise effect was now completely gone and the dice was cast – from then on it was a make-or-break situation for the 18th VGD.

December 16, 1944: setbacks on the first day

On December 16th, the two regiments of the 18th VGD on the right flank advanced quietly towards Roth from four o'clock in the morning, each led by a special assault company. If the forests and the fog did not obscure their movements, the pitch-black darkness before dawn did. The moon did not offer much light, because it had just begun its waxing crescent phase. That's how the Germans infiltrated through the American lines, leaving pockets of resistance behind them in order to achieve deep penetration and cut off the American front units from their supply and communication lines. This way of operating was more reminiscent of the German stormtroopers of the First World War than the mechanized warfare of the Second World War. Anyway, it worked for the 18th VGD, as that day the main force of the division on the right flank broke through the American battle line and advanced a total of five kilometers (3.1 miles).

American soldiers dug in in an Ardennes forest.

Despite this modest success, the main force's advance was also plagued by bad luck. For example, due to the thick fog, the 294th Regiment marched to Krewinkel in the north instead of Weckerath to the west. This kind of mistakes caused frustration among officers and fatigue among the men, who had to walk back with a full pack in sub-zero temperature conditions. On the other hand, the 295th Regiment made good progress and with the help of the StuG-Brigade 244, and the American defense of Roth was pushed aside. The poor road network of country roads in this sector prevented the infantry from being supported by heavy weapons such as mortars or accelerate their advance with trucks or even jeeps. So it was purely down to the infantry on foot with the help of the StuGs.

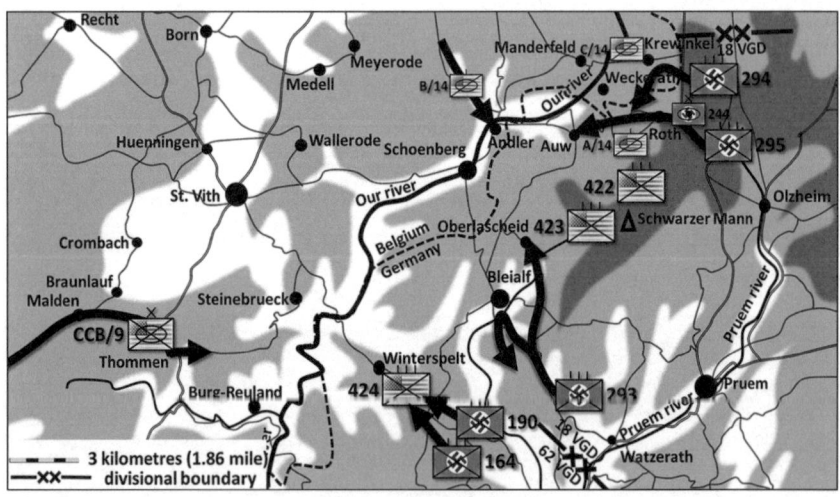

The movements of the 18th VGD and subordinated units on the first day of the Ardennes offensive.

Around noon the Germans took possession of the town of Auw. This advance could not be exploited before the elimination of the remaining Americans in Roth and Kobscheid, which could threaten the vital supply road between Roth and Auw. This took precious time. Meanwhile the nervousness in the division HQ increased, especially because it remained so quiet on the Schneifel. Operations officer Dietrich Moll was afraid that the American troops in the Schneifel had already begun their retreat or were preparing a counterattack to close the gap at Roth. In the afternoon he therefore ordered the training company, which covered the front in front of the Schneifel, to conduct a reconnaissance of the American lines to check whether the Americans were still there. These patrols were welcomed with a hail of bullets. The Americans were still on the Schneifel and would remain there for the time being. So far, so good for the Germans.

In the south, the division's third regiment, the 293rd, had suffered a setback. In the morning the advance had gone well with the capture of Oberlascheid, but in the afternoon the regiment became stuck in the woods and failed to capture its objective of the day, the town of Bleialf. A determined American counterattack threw the German troops out of the village. This meant that the Germans had to bivouac in the damp and cold forest for the night, rather than in the warm houses of Bleialf. The 18th VGD's setbacks paled however in comparison to the lack of success of the neighboring Ist SS-Panzer Corps. Despite the aforementioned massive artillery bombardment and the numerical superiority in tanks and manpower, the SS-panzercorps failed to break through the American lines on the first day. This also caused headaches for the 18th VGD, whose right flank was not covered by the advance of the SS. Hoffmann decided to continue his own advance regardless, perhaps expecting the SS to catch up the next day.

The irony was that the relative success of the 18th VGD and the failure of the Ist SS-Panzercorps on the first day of the Ardennes offensive contributed to the U.S. military leadership's initial assessment that the German offensive was local affair to destroy the bulge of the front line around the Schneifel in the sector of the 106th ID. Hodges, the commander of the U.S. 1st Army, therefore decided to support this division by sending the available mobile reserves of the American 7th and 9th Armoured Divisions to this sector instead of blocking the advance of the Ist SS Armored Corps. So it was the volksgrenadiers and not the Waffen-SS armoured troops which worried the American army leadership most at that time.

The Americans were also struggling with internal problems that day, which would have far-reaching consequences for the course of the battle. There was poor communication between the HQ of the 106th ID and its parent VIII Corps, for example. Corps Commander Middleton had told

Jones that the regiments should remain on the Schneifel until the situation became untenable. With this order, Middleton thought he had given Jones a mandate to withdraw when necessary, but Jones instead assumed that Middleton wanted to hold on to the Schneifel. At this important moment, the experienced Middleton left the decision to withdraw to the relatively inexperienced Jones. However, how could Jones know when a situation became "untenable"? The troops on the Schneifel itself were after all not involved in major battles at that time.

StuG advancing on the muddy tracks in the Ardennes, a reality in the sector of the 18th VGD.

The rather inflexible attitude of Middleton towards the Schneifel heights is quite remarkable in the light of the unfolding crisis in his frontsector. His overstretched forces were attacked along the whole line of contact and even under these circumstances the retreat of an exposed concentration of forces to more defendable positions was not even contemplated. A retreat behind the Our river would have given the inexperienced forces of the 106th ID a defensive barrier the Germans could not cross without incurring heavy losses. It also would have shortened the frontline, freeing up several battalions in the process to bolster the frontline elsewhere. In any case the Schneifel heights no longer had strategic value in a situation where the American lines in the neighbouring sectors were in the danger of being overrun, especially because no important roads ran across it. Still Middleton was reluctant to cede it to the enemy. It was all the more remarkable that he did see the danger for St. Vith crossroads.

The planned concentration of the American tank divisions in St. Vith did not bode well for the 18th VGD. The American 7th Armoured Division (further: AD) was still in its camp near Maastricht at that time and would not move to St. Vith until the morning of December 17th, but major general Jones of the 106th ID had Combat Command B (CCB) of the 9th AD at his disposal. This was the American equivalent of the German *Kampfgruppe*, namely a battlegroup consisting of units from various branches – tanks, infantry, artillery, engineers and anti-aircraft troops. He decided not to deploy this unit to avert the threat to his main force on the Schneifel, but to strengthen the 424th Regiment against the attack of the 62nd VGD at Winterspelt. In retrospect, this turned out to be a blunder, as it gave the 18th VGD the necessary respite to complete the encirclement of the Schneifel from the north. Jones assumed that the German main thrust would come from the southeast, while it was actually coming from the northeast.

Major General Troy H. Middleton in the Ardennes during the Battle of the Bulge.

December 17, 1944: the Schneifel trap closes

In the early morning of December 17th, Hoffmann decided to personally lead the advance of the 294th Regiment via field roads and snow-covered fields to the hamlet of Andler on the river Our. Once in Andler, he joined his offensive reserve, *Kampfgruppe Rennhack* (an improvised battle group named after its commander), consisting of the fusilier company and the engineer battalion, which had followed the 294th that morning. Kampfgruppe Rennhack then advanced via the paved road in the Our valley, supported by the StuG-Brigade 244. This advance went well and before noon this force arrived in Schoenberg. In the meantime, the 295th Regiment had succeeded in eliminating the American pockets of resistance in the rear and this enabled supply columns to reach the bulk of the division, which by now deep in the rear of the American 106th ID. The biggest success of the day was the capture of the undamaged bridges over the Our, an indispensable asset for any advance to St. Vith.

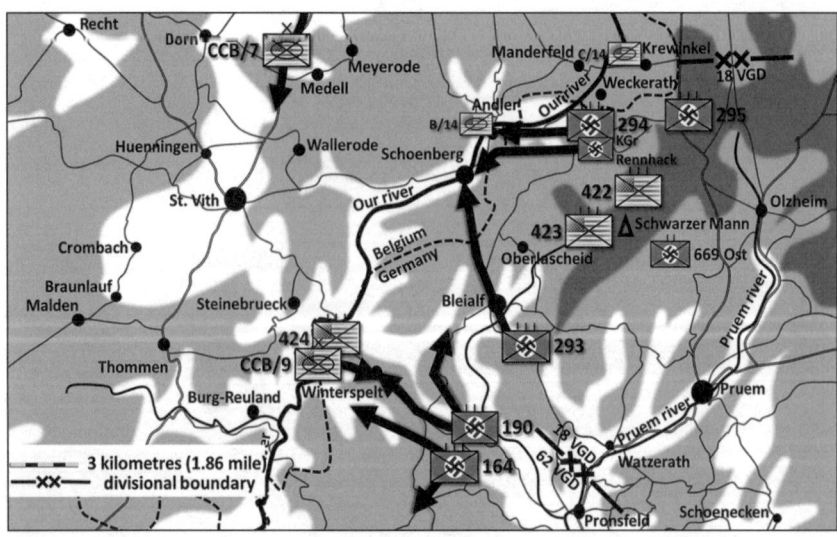

The situation and disposition of the German and American units on December 17th.

In the meantime, the left flank with the 293rd Regiment had also started the day well. The town of Bleialf was stormed by the volksgrenadiers, who broke with a dashing attack through the improvised defense by elements of the American 423rd Regiment, one of the regiments on the Schneifel. Early in the afternoon the first elements of the 293rd Regiment arrived in Schoenberg, where they found their divisional commander. Now the net around the Schneifel was basically closed. At that moment it was no longer possible for the Americans to withdraw via the bridges over the Our. Nevertheless, some Americans on the Schneifel realized the dire situation they were in, and small groups tried to force their way west towards the positions of the 424th Regiment around Winterspelt.

German heavy Tiger tanks of Kampfgruppe Peiper. They were behind schedule when the advance began.

The 18th VGD had achieved its first operational objective in the Ardennes offensive within two days. To put this into perspective, on the second day the spearhead of the 6th Panzerarmy, Joachim Peiper's SS-tankcolumn (further: Kampfgruppe Peiper), began the first day of its advance after the false start on December 16th. The officers of the 18th VGD were surprised and relieved by the complete success of the daring plan of their daredevil commander. The aforementioned Chief of

Staff Dietrich Moll testified after the war that he was surprised that the Americans did virtually nothing to stop the German advance. It is indeed striking that no counterstrikes were carried out, or that no precautions were undertaken to prepare the bridges for demolition to prevent them from falling into German hands. The scope of the Ardennes offensive must have been clear by now.

Moll only spoke for his own division by the way. On December 17th the 62nd VGD, the sister division of the 18th VGD, suffered a major setback when the Americans organized a counterattack with the aforementioned CCB of the 9th AD, supported by the artillery of the 106th ID. They ripped into the lines of the German infantry, which suffered heavy losses as a result. The German stormtroop companies were decimated and the American attack knocked out the impetus of the 62nd VGD, which had hoped to beat their sister-division in an advance to St. Vith. At the end of the day major general Jones decided to withdraw the CCB and the volksgrenadiers of the 62nd were able to catch their breath and enjoy a good night's rest after this traumatic day. The division, like its sister division, had been re-established in the autumn of 1944, but unlike its sister division, had not come into action earlier. The American counterattack with the lethal combination of tanks and artillery must have shocked the inexperienced German soldiers to the bone.

Despite their success of the Schoenberg the 18th VGD missed the opportunity to take St. Vith on the same day. The American defense was in disarray and major general Jones was basically burnt-out. Dispirited, he handed over the defense of the town to brigadier general Bruce C. Clarke (1901-1988), commander of the CCB of the 7th

General Bruce C. Clarke, the commander who took charge of the American troops in St. Vith.

AD. Clarke was at the vanguard of his troops, but he did not yet have any units in St. Vith to effectively defend the place. Apart from some rearguard troops, including engineer units, there were no combat troops between Schoenberg and St. Vith. The Germans had come within a few kilometers of the town, but they had no idea that the town was virtually undefended.

Samuel Mitcham, in his book about the Ardennes offensive (Panzers in Winter, 2006), speaks of a missed golden opportunity for the Germans to take St. Vith on December 17th. I personally think that although the 18th VGD had achieved success, the division was then also in a vulnerable position. The Germans were overstretched at this point and had no heavy weapons to breach a determined defense of St. Vith. The troops were spread over a large area and there were American troop concentrations in the vicinity of Schoenberg, such as in Winterspelt and on the Schneifel, which could easily turn the odds in favor of the Americans, if they would launch a determined attack. Although the two American regiments on the Schneifel were cut off from supplies, they were still a formidable force. Moreover, the heavy weapons of the 18th VGD were still on their way, as the Ardennes country roads had turned into a mud pit due to the heavy traffic. The question is also whether the vanguard of the division could have held on to St. Vith, when the American 7th AD would launch an attack on the town.

Hoffmann used the spell in the offensive in his sector to issue new orders and redeploy his troops for the next stage. He realized that the division now had to combine two tasks, namely the elimination of the American troops on the Scheifel and the advance to St. Vith. He therefore split the command of the division in two – his operations officer Moll would deal with the two American regiments on the Schneifel, while he himself would focus on the capture of St. Vith. Moll received two regiments (293rd and 295th), the divisional artillery, all units from the troop and reinforcement from the 669th East-Battalion for his task. The latter was a unit consisting of former prisoners of war from Soviet-Russia, who were now in German military service. This meant that Hoffmann himself only had the 294th Regiment, the engineer battalion, the fusilier company and

Sturmgeschuetz-Brigade 244. In other words, the Germans expected the Americans on the Schneifel to be a tough nut to crack.

American tanks in the winter weather. The 7th Armoured Division came to the rescue of the 106th ID.

Among the American ranks of the 106th ID morale was dropping that day. It became clear on the Schneifel that they were cut off. Supplies and mail were no longer coming in and communications by radio were becoming irregular. James W. Gardner, who served in the HQ company of the 422nd Regiment's 2nd Battalion, worded in hindsight his feelings as follows: "The last communication from Division Headquarters was received (I think the 18th). We knew we were cut off. No supplies could be dropped because the weather was too bad. It was a matter of us getting pulverized. Our big guns had been silenced and we were at the mercy of theirs." The lack of communications seemed to be the worst part – no air- or artillerysupport could be called in anymore. The chain of command was eroding and the Americans were largely left to their own devices on the snowy heights.

December 18, 1944: the Americans strike back

Immediately after the encirclement of the Americans on the Schneifel, the situation was very confusing for all parties involved. The Germans were plagued by the aforementioned groups of Americans who tried to push their way west. However, these were not only stragglers, but also entire units of Americans who did not know exactly where the Germans were at that moment. On the night of December 17th to 18th, the motorized column of the American 589th Field Artillery Battalion attempted to force its way west through Schoenberg. The forward battery was ambushed and completely destroyed. The other batteries did not fare much better and only remnants of the battalion managed to escape the German fire through the darkness. Arthur C. Brown of the HQ battery remembers his escape as follows: "Arming ourselves with M1 Garand rifles, we prepared to set out to regain our lines. As there were Germans on the road in front of the house, we made our way undetected to the west end of the village [of Born]. There we entered a house to seek directions of the householders. Fortunately the people were friendly, and sent us on our way with some food and a bottle of wine."

The American regiments on the Schneifel had remained where they were until then, much to the surprise of the Germans. On December 18th, major general Jones finally ordered them to turn around and launch a major attack on Schoenberg. However, the Americans had the greatest difficulty moving en masse – trucks and jeeps turned the snow-covered roads into a sea of mud and they became stuck. It was not until dusk that the American 423rd Regiment was ready for the breakout. At that time, the Germans had already beenin firm control of Schoenberg for more than 24 hours and had plenty of time to put the village in a state of defense. When it kicked off the American attack was greeted with a storm of machine gun fire and shells. The American commander of the vanguard was killed, and a subsequent German counterattack finally put an end to the first attempt to break the encirclement. Harry C. McKinley remembered: "Upon our attack on Schoenberg we were faced on all sides by Germans with all types and sizes of guns and ammunition. (...) This horrible beating from explosions in all directions and overhead with the concussions was more than I now believe anyone could possibly go through. But, by some God given power, I stayed alive."

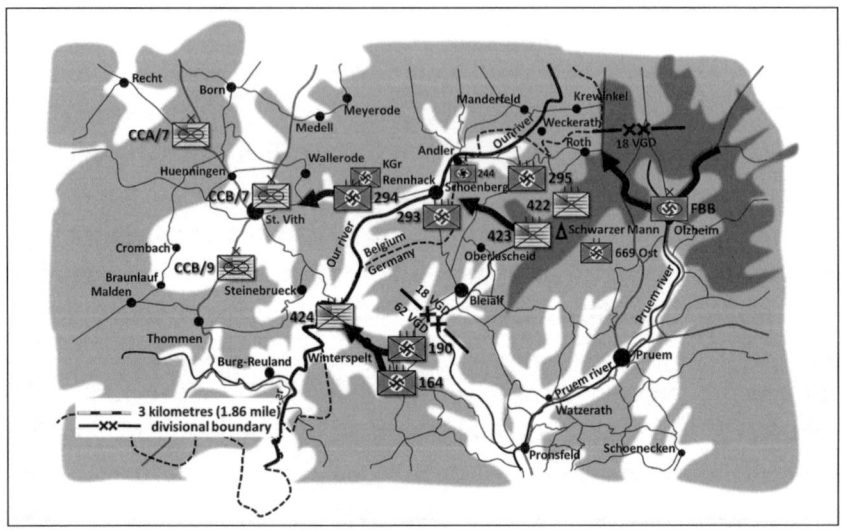

Military situation on December 18th.

The question is whether the Americans really did not do anything to relieve the surrounded regiments from outside, or at least to supply them from the air. The latter had indeed been requested in the afternoon of December 17th, but the transport aircraft did not arrive in Belgium until the next day and ultimately the mission was canceled because no escort aircraft were available to defend against possible German aircraft. This was quite remarkable because the German Luftwaffe had basically suspended frontline air support for almost half a year by now. Even if the transportplanes would take off, it remained questionable whether the planes would have been able to drop supplies accurately given the absence of clear landmarks in the landscape. Moreover, the Germans were busy tightening the noose around the encirclement. It was however important for morale of the encircled troops to let them know that everything was done to relieve them, or at least to get supplies in.

American artillery was an important asset in the defense of the lines in the Ardennes.

In the meantime, the American 7th AD had arrived in St. Vith and set up a defensive perimeter around the town. The remains of the 106th ID, including the 424th Regiment, withdrew within this defensive ring, which had the shape of a horseshoe. The Americans were defending St. Vith, even though the German spearheads to the left and right of St. Vith had penetrated deep behind the American lines. The British Field Marshall Bernhard L. Montgomery had ordered the town to be defended as long as possible. He had taken command of the northern flank of what had taken the shape of a bulge in the American lines and he immediately saw the strategic value of St. Vith. The road junction of St. Vith was vital to any German advance from the Ardennes to the west.

On the German side, the lack of St. Vith as a traffic artery was strongly felt. Since the 1st SS-Panzer Corps had failed to break through the American lines on the Elsenborn Ridge, where the aforementioned American 2nd ID had bolstered the line. The SS-Panzerdivisions now had to move west through the narrow border corridor at Losheim. The result was a huge traffic jam. Things were not much different in the sector of the LXVI Corps, where the 18th and 62nd VGDs were facing similar problems although they had much less motorized vehicles. The army trucks had to move over a limited road network and the artillery also had to be brought forward along the same road. On December 18th, the Volksgrenadiers still could not count on the support of their heavy artillery during their advance to St. Vith as a result.

An American soldier reloading his rifle after a failed German attack.

Originally, the German attack on St. Vith was planned for December 18th, with the VGDs of the LXVI Corps supported by the *Fuehrer-Begleit-Brigade* (Fuehrer Escort Brigade, further: FBB). The core of the FBB was formed by Adolf Hitler's former escort troops (when he still visited enemy territory). It was commanded by the die-hard national-socialist colonel Otto Ernst Remer (1912-1997), who had been instrumental in quelling the officer-coup in Berlin on July 20th 1944. His brigade was a heavily armed unit which included Panzer IV tanks and StuGs. These tanks and assault guns were necessary to give the volksgrenadiers a fighting chance against the American 7th AD. The FBB therefore also had to use the same routes as the supply of the LXVI Corps, which worsened the traffic jams, because its tanks ran out of fuel due to the strain on motors as they had to plough through the mud. Remer calls later the conditions as follows: "The road of advance ordered was completely jammed and in a bad condition. Travelling

Otto Ernst Remer, the officer who commanded the Fuehrer Begleit Brigade who supported the attack on St. Vith.

off the road was impossible, even for track-laying vehicles. I therefore reckoned with a considerable delay of the march movement and reported this to the armycorps." These delays meant that the attack against the American 7th AD in St. Vith had to be postponed until further notice.

December 19, 1944: the last American convulsion on the Schneifel

The arrival of the 7th AD did not bring the 106th ID the relief the Americans needed to save their regiments on the Schneifel. On December 19th, the 7th AD was in danger of being surrounded itself in the region around St. Vith. On the left flank, Kampfgruppe Peiper from the 1st SS-Panzerdivision had advanced towards Stoumont and on the right flank the LVIII Panzercorps had reached Houffalize that day. The situation was so critical in the Allied camp that Montgomery decided to move his best divisions all the way from the Netherlands towards the Ardennes to protect the bridges over the Meuse against a possible German breakthrough. In the dead of winter the troops were loaded into trucks and moved in an arduous journey over icy roads to the Ardennes.

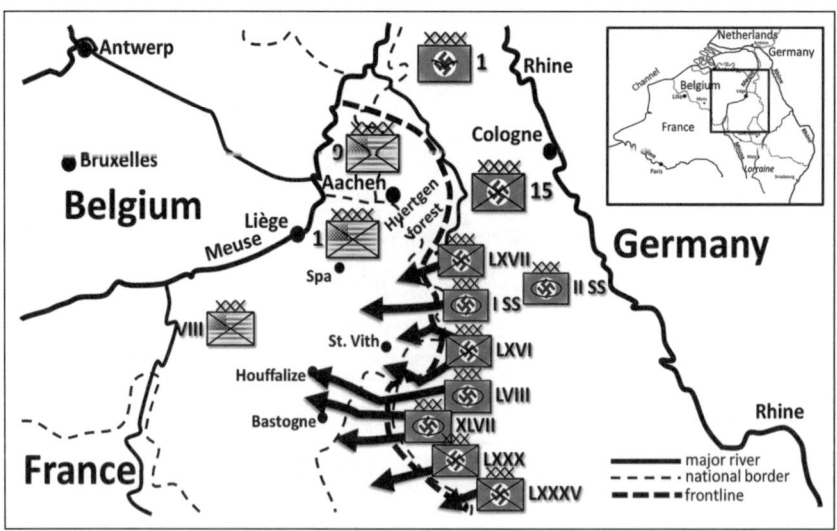

Strategic situation in the Ardennes on December 19th 1944.

In the meantime, the American troops on the Schneifel made a last attempt to break out to St. Vith. After the failure of the 423rd regiment's attack on December 18th, the 422nd regiment in turn attempted to capture

Schoenberg and advance west on the morning of December 19th. The entire regiment was thrown into battle, but the Germans knew since the American attack the previous day that Schoenberg was the primary target of a possible breakout from the Schneifel. As a result, the Americans soon came under fire from German machine guns and artillery from all sides. To make matters worse, StuGs also appeared and used high explosive shells against the exposed American infantry. The American attack was skillfully broken up and the Germans took several thousand prisoners.

German officers are reading maps, which were indispensable in the misty landscape with few road signs.

This failed attack on Schoenberg was the beginning of the end for the surrounded American regiments on the Schneifel. The troops were constantly under fire from German artillery, supplies of ammunition and food were depleted and there was hardly any contact with division HQ. At that time, the regiments were also scattered in the region, exposed to the winter weather, as a result of abandoning their positions. The men probably gave a demoralized impression at that moment after leaving their quarters, the failed attacks and the lack of air supply. One can imagine that the soldiers felt that they had been abandoned. The regimental commanders therefore decided the same day to surrender the troops to the Germans to prevent further unnecessary losses. Sergeant Francis Kelly recalls that he and his comrades were hungry and thirsty. Once on the march his battalion soon lost cohesion and disintegrated into a mob. Officers did not know what to do and did not bother to screen the battalion with scouts. After a token firefight, the battalion surrendered to the Germans.

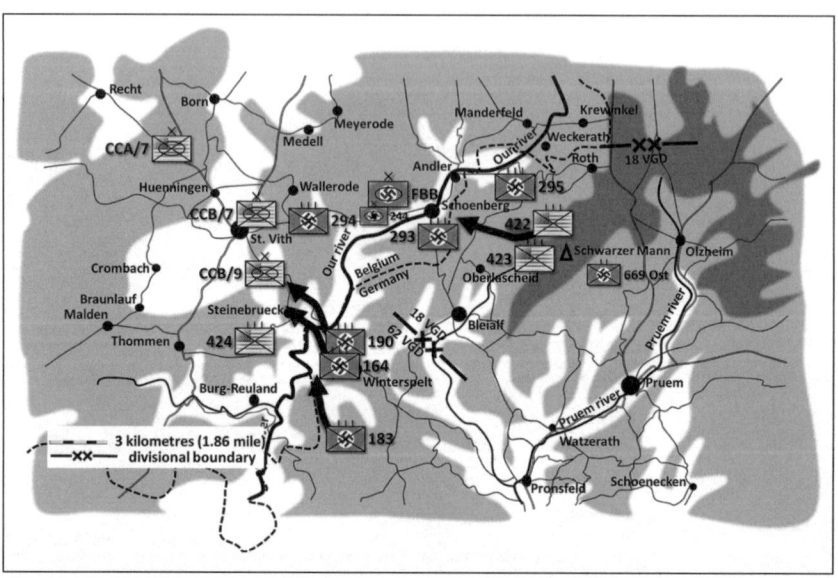

Situation on the Eiffel front sector on December 19th.

Luitenant L. Martin Jones painted an even bleaker picture of the state of the American troops. According to him, the hungry and exhausted

troops received the order to surrender with a remarkable relief with the expectation that the deprivations would be over soon. Anything looked better than the sorry state they were in. They probably just craved for food, a warm shelter, and a good night's rest. In any case they were ripe for surrender. After conveying the regimental decision to

Alan W. Jones was an exhausted and broken man after losing most of his command in three days.

lay down their arms, the captain of G-company said that anyone who wanted could try to reach the American lines and promptly ran off in the western direction. He apparently did not expect anybody from his outfit to follow him, a sure sign of a lack of authority. His demoralized company surrendered at the first opportunity.

In total, the Germans captured an estimated 8,000 soldiers on and near the Schneifel. This was almost the entire strength of the 18th VGD, which at the time was estimated to have just under 9,000 soldiers. Hoffmann's daring plan was a complete success and the American 106th Division was almost completely wiped off the map. The Germans were very surprised that the regiments on the Schneifel had surrendered so quickly. A shock wave also went through the American ranks. Corps commander Middleton was used to some setbacks those days, as his armycorps was attacked by the entire 5th Panzerarmy, but the surrender of two regiments after just four days of fighting was a bit too much. It became also too much for major general Jones two days later – he suffered a heart attack and was relieved of command to recover. He never commanded a unit in the field again.

American prisoners of war are being brought back to the rear.

The surrender of the American troops in the Schneifel was good news for the 18th VGD. Now two regiments of infantry and divisional artillery were released to be deployed in the capture of St. Vith. However, it would take at least another day before these troops would have taken their attack positions near St. Vith – the German troops moved on foot and their artillery was largely horse-drawn. In the meantime, the 294th Regiment attempted to storm St. Vith around noon, but this attack was broken up by American artillery when the Germans advanced into open terrain. Colonel Remer remarked dryly: "The attack of the 18 VGD, which was commenced with only weak artillery, did not lead to any success." In the evening, Hoffmann reported that the attack had been repulsed with heavy losses by superior enemy forces. This was even more proof that the vanguard had to wait for the rest of the division before an attack towards St. Vith could be launched. It also proved that the original plan to capture St. Vith on the third day of the offensive had been a very optimistic plan.

Remer's armour of the FBB did not fare much better against the defenses of the 7th AD, which were ready and waiting for him: "The armored point of my advanced detachment, which had, during this, advanced approximately to the bend of the road north of Pruemerberg, received rather strong anti-tank fire. The company attacking through the woods south of the road was repelled with heavy losses by very well-placed enemy artillery fire." St. Vith could not be taken anymore by a stealthy vanguard, a possibility which presented itself the previous day. As a result December 20th was dedicated in bringing forward the necessary troops, artillery and supplies for a concerted attack against the American positions around the town. December 19th had been the day the struggle of the 106th ID was largely over, and that of the 7th AD was just about to begin.

December 21, 1944: main objective St. Vith

The importance of St. Vith for both sides cannot be underestimated. For the Germans it was a crucial road junction for the advance west, but for a while the Americans regarded it as a springboard for their own counterattack. They considered an attack from St. Vith towards Malmédy in order to encircle and completely destroy the 1st, 2nd and 9th SS-Panzer Divisions. On a map it seemed a good idea, but thankfully for the 7th AD they never the order to attack in that direction, because the Germans were about to attack the 7th AD from multiple dirctions. St. Vith had grown considerably in significance following the first days of the Ardennes offensive.

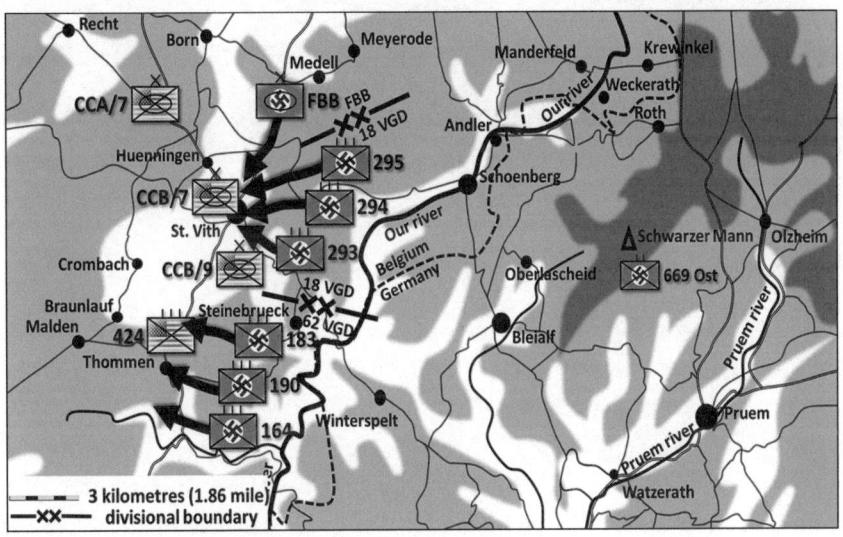

Situation on the Eiffel front sector on December 21st.

Field Marshal Walter Model (1891-1945), commander of Army Group B, and Hasso von Manteuffel (1897-1978), commander of the 5th Panzerarmy, visited the HQ of the 18th VGD on December 20th. This high-ranking visit was however not to congratulate the division commander on his spectacular success in the Schneifel, but to question him as to why St. Vith had not yet been captured. They had reasons to be frustrated because Bastogne, the other major crossroads in the 5th Panzerarmy's sector, had not yet been taken. This caused the Germans to encounter serious logistical problems, as St. Vith had by now become not only crucial for the 5th Panzerarmy, but also for 6th Panzerarmy. The advance of the Ist SS-Panzercorps had been stopped in its tracks and now the 6th Panzerarmy had to reroute south and advance through the sector of the 5th Panzerarmy to bring troops westward. Hoffmann was ordered to attack St. Vith with all available troops. Apparently he managed to stand his ground against his superiors, because he convinced them not to press the attack until he had properly deployed his troops and artillery, which was the next day.

American infantry during the winter of 1944-45. Few soldiers managed to escape the German encirclement in the Schneifel.

In retrospect, it is remarkable that the capture of an important traffic junction such as St. Vith, which was also in the middle of the German advance into the Ardennes, was assigned to the weakest corps of the 5th Panzerarmy, which consisted of only two unassuming VGDs. Even in this hour of greatest need, the LXVI Corps was only reinforced with the aforementioned FBB, which was only a brigade and had only one battalion of tanks. Yet this relatively small unit managed to scare the hell out of the Americans, as the men belonged to the so-called Großdeutschland troops

(Großdeutschland: Greater Germany, further: GD). These were troops originally specially selected to serve in the Berlin city garrison, but also in the elite GD Armoured Division. This division consisted for a large part of hand-picked troops and had originally three tank battalions on the roster: one for Panzer IV, one for Panther, and one for Tiger tanks. The FBB men were also allowed to wear the GD-insignia, like the armband, which made the Americans initially think they were being attacked by no less than the GD Armoured Division itself.

On December 21st, German general Walter Lucht, commander of LXVI Corps, gathered his commanders and urged them that St. Vith had to be conquered that day at all cost. At eleven o'clock in the morning, all tubes of the available artillery units opened fire on the American positions, after which the volksgrenadiers and soldiers from the FBB stormed the lines. Initially they were not successful. The Americans managed to hold the line and inflict heavy losses on the Germans. However, the Germans did not simply give up on that day – attack after attack followed. These attacks hit the American lines like waves and just like with the coastline, every attack wave chipped away the American defenses.

The storming of St. Vith on December 21st is always presented in American literature as a battle against titans, with Tiger tanks appearing everywhere. In reality the Germans had to contend themselves with a couple of dozen Panzer IV tanks and StuGs. I found the most grotesque description of the German attack on St. Vith in Patrick Delaforce's book *Battle of the Bulge* (2004, 151), in which he paints a picture of Tiger and Panther tanks that rolled into the town loaded with volksgrenadiers on the back of the tanks. In reality it was a handful of StuGs, the remaining vehicles of StuG-Brigade 244 after almost a week in continuous action, that supported an attack by the 18th VGD on St-Vith at around five o'clock at nightfall.

The StuGs fulfilled their original purpose and provided direct artillery support to the infantry. They literally shot the American infantry out of their foxholes, while the American local commander frantically called general Clarke, the aforementioned American garrison commander of St. Vith, for tank destroyers. These were specialized American tanks purposely built to destroy German tanks. In the meantime the night had fallen and the Americans were also attacked elsewhere along the frontline. The Americans in this front sector therefore had to do without tank support. The 18th VGD thus broke through the American line after nightfall. Field Marshal Von Rundstedt, the German commander-in-chief on the Western Front, did not want any respite and at half past seven in the evening he was on the phone to insist that St. Vith be taken the very same day. The very success of the Ardennes offensive was at that moment depending on Hoffmann's volksgrenadiers.

German infantry advancing in the forest, armed with Sturmgewehr 44.

The soldiers of the 18th VGD thus resumed their attack on St. Vith. The American general Clarke saw the writing on the wall and preferred an organised retreat over a rout. At half past ten he gave the order to evacuate St. Vith and set up a new defensive line west of the town. This tactical retreat had major consequences. The loss of St. Vith was the beginning of the end of the American horseshoe-shaped defensive perimeter that had been set up since December 18th to halt the German offensive and had become a thorn in the side of the German advance for both panzerarmies. For the Germans the capture of St. Vith seemed to open up new opportunities for their offensive. It enabled the 6th Panzerarmy to deploy the II SS-Panzercorps towards Werbomont in an effort to relieve Kampfgruppe Peiper and reinvigorate their attempt to reach the Meuse after all. It also alleviated the logistical issues of 5th Panzerarmy, which never managed to capture the Bastogne crossroads, and allowed it to bring forward troops and supplies for a dash to the Meuse. In hindsight all in vain, but both parties did not know that at the time.

StuG in action during winter on the Eastern Front. It gives a good impression of the conditions similar to those in the Ardennes.

The capture of St. Vith had totally exhausted the 18th VGD. After a week of continuous fighting on foot in sub-zero temperatures through hills and forests, the combat units had suffered serious losses and the soldiers were exhausted. The division had however not totally lost its capability to strike as they managed to book one last success on December 24th by capturing Poteau, a village that had been attacked in vain for days by the vanguard of the 9th SS-Panzerdivision. The volksgrenadiers had not only bested their Wehrmacht comrades of the GD-troops but even the Waffen-SS. The division did however never totally recover from its losses in the Ardennes. By mid-January 1945 the division was completely depleted in terms of manpower, and two months later the division was officially disbanded.

General Hoffmann-Schoenborn had by then already left the division. In February 1945 he got the position he had aspired in 1944 – the command of a panzerdivision. Three months later the war was over.

Conclusion

The 18th VGD came to the Eifel under a different star than the 106th ID. The former was fully aware that the Americans could take the offensive at any time. The commander was also aware of the strengths and weaknesses of his unit and made every effort to prepare the division for its tasks, both defensive and offensive. The latter division went to the front under the impression that it was a quiet sector and that it was not necessary to take precautions against an enemy attack. Although both divisions had to defend an extensive front line, the 106th ID made the mistake of concentrating two of its three regiments in a relatively small sector of the front. This clustering looked more like positioning for an offensive than a defense.

In American literature, the Battle of the Bulge is usually depicted as an attack by an initial overwhelming force. Although this was along most of the frontline, this was not the case in the sector of the 18th VGD. The image of Panther and Tiger tanks that plowed through the American lines accompanied by hordes of Volksgrenadiers is incorrect. The 18th VGD's operation was mainly an infantry attack, bypassing American resistance pockets by means of infiltration tactics. The 18th VGD was quantitatively and qualitatively inferior to the American 106th ID. The division had to encircle the main force of the American division as quickly as possible by means of a smart and daring attack plan. She was supported by just over a dozen StuGs. The cooperation between these assault guns and the infantry was however the specialty of major general Hoffmann-Schoenborn, who had been a commander of an assault gun unit with remarkable distinction earlier in the war.

The demise of the American 106th ID is attributed to a whole list of factors, of which poor communication and inexperienced men are the most mentioned. However, communication could not be the only factor in the failure of command. What is striking is that not only the division commander, but also his subordinates did not exactly excel in initiative. The image of the division during the Battle of the Bulge is that of a rabbit standing in the middle of the road looking into the headlights of an oncoming car. American officers of new divisions were often as green as their subordinates. While the inexperienced 18th VGD was led by experienced officers and had a cadre of veterans, the officers of the 106th ID were hardly prepared for what awaited them on the ground. The historiography places too much emphasis on the condition of the men of the 106th ID, and too little on the failure of command at divisional and regimental level.

The 106th ID was poorly positioned and poorly led, but the American division also failed to hinder the Germans in their operations. There was no counterattack, and the low point was the failure to blow up the bridge over the Our at Schoenberg. The complete capture of the Our Bridge was one of the biggest successes of the 18th VGD, especially in the light of the setbacks of neighbouring Kampfgruppe Peiper, which saw almost all the bridges blown up one by one in front of its nose. This success enabled the division to bring its artillery, including the StuGs, into position for the capture of St. Vith. It is unlikely that the division could have mounted a successful attack on the town without this artillery support. In addition, the infantry also had to be supplied with rations and ammunition across this bridge.

The 18th VGD brought the operation around the Schneifel to a successful conclusion, but the planned capture of St. Vith on the third day was clearly a bridge too far. The division was so successful that the Americans directed their available mobile reinforcements to St. Vith. The division still had its hands full with the encirclement of the American forces on the Schneifel, which involved two of its three regiments. Ultimately, the division could only continue their attack on St. Vith after the surrender of the Americans on the Schneifel, a clear underestimation of this task when planning the offensive. Nevertheless, the 18th VGD finally managed to break the American line at St. Vith on the evening of December 21, achieving its strategic objective. In retrospect, the battle for the Schneifel and the capture of St. Vith was the first and last achievement of the 18th VGD. In this perspective the Ardennes offensive did not only mean the demise of the American 106th ID, but also the German 18th VGD. Their success of capturing St. Vith was however eclipsed by subsequent events and the usual focus on the armoured divisions in the post-war historiography of the Ardennes offensive.

Former commander Bruce C. Clarke and Hasso von Manteuffel meet up in the Ardennes in 1965. No such meeting took place with Hoffmann-Schoenborn.

Literature

Leo Barron, *Patton at the Battle of the Bulge: How the General's Tanks Turned the Tide at Bastogne* (Penguin 2014).

Christer Bergstroem, *The Ardennes 1944-1945, Hitler's Winter Offensive* (Casemat Publishers 2014).

William C. C. Cavanagh en Karl Cavanagh, *A Tour of the Bulge Battlefields* (Pen & Sword 2001).

Bruce C. Clarke, The Battle of St. Vith, Belgium, 17-23 December 1944; an Historical Example of Armor in the Defense (U.S. Army Armor School 1969).

Bruce C. Clarke, 'The Battle for St. Vith: Armor in the Defense and Delay', in: *Armor* november-december 1974.

Hugh M. Cole, *The Ardennes – the Battle of the Bulge* [United States Army in World War II, The European Theater of Operations] (U.S. Army Center of Military History 1964).

Jack Didden & Maarten Swarts, *The Army that got away – The German 15. Armee in the Summer of 1944* (Zwaardvisch 2022).

Richard Ernest Dupuy, *St. Vith Lion in the Way. The 106th Infantry Division in World Way II* (Infantry Journal Press 1949).

David R. Durr, *The cadre division concept – the 106th Infantry Division revisited* (U.S. Army War College 1992).

Charles Glass, *The Deserters. A Hidden History of World War II* (Penguin Publishers 2013).

Bart Howard, 'Saddles and Sabers: 70 Years On – Battle of St. Vith', in: *Armor* (October-December 2014).

Franz Kurowski, *Panther nach vorn! Mit der Panzer-Lehr-Division bis zum bitteren Ende* (Pour le mérite 2014).

Paul St.Laurent, Charles Crow, Johnny Everette, Gregory Fontenot, Robert V. Hester, Thomas D.MacIver, M.A.H.Al-zayad'Sajd, Emerson H. Morgan, *The Battle of St. Vith* (Combat Studies Institute 1984).

Charles B. MacDonald, *The Siegfried Line Campaign* (Center of Military History, U.S. Army 1963).

Samuel L.A. Marshall, *Bastogne: the story of the first eight days in which the 101st Airborne Division was closed within the ring of German forces.* (Infantry journal Press, 1946).

John C. McManus, *Alamo in the Ardennes: The Untold Story of the American Soldiers Who Made the Defense of Bastogne Possible* (John Wiley and Sons 2007).

Samuel W. Mitcham, *Panzers in Winter. Hitler's Army and the Battle of the Bulge* (Stackpole Military History Series 2006).

J.D. Morelock, *Generals of the Ardennes. American Leadership in the Battle of the Bulge* (National Defense University Press 1994).

Douglas E. Nash, *Victory Was Beyond Their Grasp: With the 272nd Volks-Grenadier Division from the Hurtgen Forest to the Heart of the Reich* (Aberjona Press 2008).

John Nelson Rickard, 'December 1944: Eisenhower, Bradley, and the Calculated Risk in the Ardennes' in: *Global War Studies* 8-1 (2011) 7-34.

Bruce Quarrie, *The Ardennes Offensive. V Panzer Armee* (Oxford 2000).

Bill Schiller en Lisa Thompson, *75th Infantry Division: Ardennes, Central Europe, Rhineland* (Turner Publishing 1999).

Michael Tolhurst, *Saint Vith, 106th US Infantry Division* (Barnsley 1999, tweede druk 2000).

George Winter, *Freineux and Lamormenil – the Ardennes* (J.J. Fedorowicz Publishing 1994).

Steven Zaloga, *Smashing Hitler's Panzers: The Defeat of the Hitler Youth Panzer Division in the Battle of the Bulge* (*Rowman & Littlefield* 2018).

Archive sources

Bundesarchiv, *Reichsministerium fuer Volksaufklärung und Propaganda*, File R55/601: Wöchentliche Tätigkeitsberichte des Leiters der Abteilung Propaganda – Chef des Propagandastabes – als Zusammenfassung der Berichte der Reichspropagandaämter, der Gaupropagandaleitungen sowie der Redner- und SD-Berichte.

Walter Lucht, *LXVI Corps (Oct – 23 Dec 1944)* [MS # B-333].

Walter Lucht, *The 18th Infantry Division in the Ardennes offensive* [MS A-929]

Dietrich Moll, *18th Volks Grenadier Division (1 Sep 1944 – 25 Jan 1945)* [MS # B-688].

Otto Ernst Remer, *The Führer-Begleit-Brigade in the Ardennes Offensive (16 Dec 44 to 26 Jan 45)* [MS # B-592]

Register of names

Bradley, Omar 44
Brown, Arthur C. 57
Clarke, Bruce C. 54, 55, 69, 70, 75
Delaforce, Patrick 69
Eisenhower, Dwight D. 43, 44
Gardner, James W. 56
Goering, Hermann 10
Himmler, Heinrich 13, 19
Hitler, Adolf 60
Hodges, Courtney B. 35, 49
Hoffmann-Schoenborn, Guenther
    16-22, 29-33, 38-40, 42, 46, 49, 55,
    65, 68, 72, 73
Jones, Alan W. 26, 35, 50, 51, 64, 65
Jones, L. Martin 64
Kelly, Francis 64
McKinley, Harry C. 58
Lammerding, Heinz 22, 23
Lucht, Walter 31, 69
Manteuffel, Hasso von 9, 67, 75
Middleton, Troy H. 35, 49-51, 65
Mitcham, Samuel 55
Model, Walter 67
Moll, Dietrich 15, 48, 54 55
Montgomery, Bernhard L. 59, 62
Nash, Douglas 9
Peiper, Joachim (also: Jochen) 9, 53, 62,
    71, 74
Rennhack 52
Rundstedt, Gerd von 70

Remer, Otto Ernst 60, 61, 66
Quarrie, Bruce 18
Tresckow, Joachim von 13

Register of places

Aachen 9, 28, 35
Andler 52
Auw 48
Bastogne 9, 37, 68, 71
Berlin 60, 69
Bleialf 49, 53
Caen 11
Dinant 9
Esbjerg 13
Falaise 11
Houffalize 37, 62
Kobscheid 48
Krewinkel 48
Losheim 59
Maastricht 51
Malmédy 67
Metz 35
Mons 13
Moscow 18
Oberlascheid 49
Posen (Poznań) 17
Poteau 71
Pruemerberg 66
Roth 47, 48
Rzhev 13
Salerno 35
Schoenberg 37-39, 52-55, 57, 58, 62, 63, 74
Spa 35, 43

St. Vith 9, 21, 32, 37, 39, 51, 52, 54, 55, 59-62, 66-71, 74
Stalingrad (Wolgograd) 34
Stoumont 62
Thermopylae 17
Weckerath 48
Werbomont 71
Winterspelt 51, 53, 55